DATE DUE

Reading About
THE GRIZZLY BEAR

Carol Greene

Content Consultant:
Dan Wharton, Ph.D., Curator,
New York Zoological Society

Reading Consultant:
Michael P. French, Ph.D.,
Bowling Green State University

ENSLOW PUBLISHERS, INC.

Bloy St. & Ramsey Ave.
Box 777
Hillside, N.J. 07205
U.S.A.

P.O. Box 38
Aldershot
Hants GU12 6BP
U.K.

Library of Congress Cataloging-in-Publication Data

Greene, Carol.
    Reading about the grizzly bear / Carol Greene.
       p. cm. — (Friends in danger series)
    Includes index.
    Summary: Describes the physical characteristics and behavior of
the grizzly bear and discusses some of the dangers it faces.
    ISBN 0-89490-423-X
    1. Grizzly bear—Juvenile literature. 2. Rare mammals—Juvenile
literature. [1. Grizzly bear. 2. Bears. 3. Rare animals.]
    I. Title. II. Series: Greene, Carol. Friends in danger series.
QL737.C27G7394 1993
599.74′446—dc20   92-26803
                                                      CIP
                                                      AC

Printed in the United States of America

10 9 8 7 6 5 4 3 2 1

Photo Credits: ©The Bettmann Archive, p. 22; ©Alissa Crandall/Liaison International,
pp. 14, 16; © Gerry Ellis/The Wildlife Collection, pp. 10, 20; ©Henry Holdsworth/The
Wildlife Collection, p. 18; ©Thomas Kitchin/Tom Stack & Associates, pp. 1, 4, 6; ©Tom
and Pat Leeson, p. 26; ©Tom McHugh/Photo Researchers, Inc., p. 8; ©Ron Sanford, pp.
12, 24.

Cover Photo Credit: ©Henry Holdsworth/The Wildlife Collection

Photo Researcher: Grace How

CONTENTS

BELLA

A cold wind blows
through the mountains.
Summer is almost over.
Bella leads her cubs
out to find food.
It is time to eat and eat.

A grizzly mother and her cubs.

Bella is a grizzly bear.
Thick fur keeps her
and her cubs warm.
Most grizzlies are brown.
But some are almost black
and some are the color
of a new penny.

As the bears walk along,
they look slow and clumsy.
But a grizzly can run
25 miles an hour.
That's fast.

Grizzly bears have shaggy coats.

Walking on all four paws,
an adult can be four feet tall.
Standing on its hind paws,
it can be five to nine feet tall.
Grizzlies weigh from
300 to 800 pounds.
That's big.

Bella cannot see well.
But her hearing is good
and her sense of smell
is very good.

When an adult grizzly bear stands on its
hind legs, it looks huge.

She stops and sniffs.
She smells some nuts that
a squirrel hid in a log.
Bella tears the log apart
with her sharp front claws.

A grizzly's claws can be
three to six inches long.

Bella and her cubs
eat the nuts.
But they must eat more.
So they move on.

Grizzly bears have long claws.

Next Bella smells berries.
But she smells
a male grizzly too.
She makes her cubs
stay in one place and,
carefully, she goes on.

Male grizzlies can hurt cubs.
They can even kill them.

This male is leaving.
So Bella and the cubs eat
the berries he left behind.
But they must eat more.

A grizzly bear smells danger.

They go on to a creek.
Bella reaches in and—
just like that—
grabs a fish with her paw.

She and the cubs eat
several fish.

A grizzly snatches up a fish as it swims
upstream.

She and the cubs
did not eat so much
earlier in the summer.
They slept all day
and found food at night.

But soon Bella will dig
a tunnel in a hillside.
It will lead to a den.
Bella and her cubs will
sleep in the den all winter.

A grizzly bear and her cubs look for food.

Grizzlies do not hibernate.
Hibernating animals change
while they sleep.
Their bodies slow down.

Grizzlies' bodies do not change
much while they sleep.
But they sleep a long time.
So they need lots of fat
to keep them alive.

When spring comes,
Bella and her cubs
will leave their den.
And, sure enough, they
will be hungry again.

Grizzlies eat a lot of food before winter.

DANGER!

Grizzly bears used to live
all over North America
west of the Mississippi River,
from Alaska to Mexico.

Now there are only
about 900 grizzlies left
in the lower 48 states.
Most live around Yellowstone
and Glacier National Parks.

More grizzlies still live
in Alaska and Canada.

At one time there may have been more
than 100,000 bears in the lower 48 states.

People used to kill grizzlies
for their heads, fur, and claws.
Now that is against the law.
But some people still do it.

People are also taking
the land where grizzlies live.
They dig mines, cut trees,
build buildings, raise animals,
camp, and hike.

Some people hunted grizzlies for fun.

Grizzlies do not like
to get near people.
But they can't help it when
their own places are gone.

The best way to help
grizzly bears is to leave
them and their land alone.
Even if we don't see them,
we will know they are there.

Grizzlies try to stay away from people.

WHAT YOU CAN DO

1. Learn more about grizzlies.
   Read books and watch nature
   shows.

2. Visit grizzlies at a zoo,
   if you can.

3. See if your family can
   join a group that works
   to keep wild places wild.
   Your librarian can help you
   find names of these groups.

4. *Never* go near a grizzly.
   They really are wild animals.

Grizzly cubs are cute, but they are
dangerous, too.

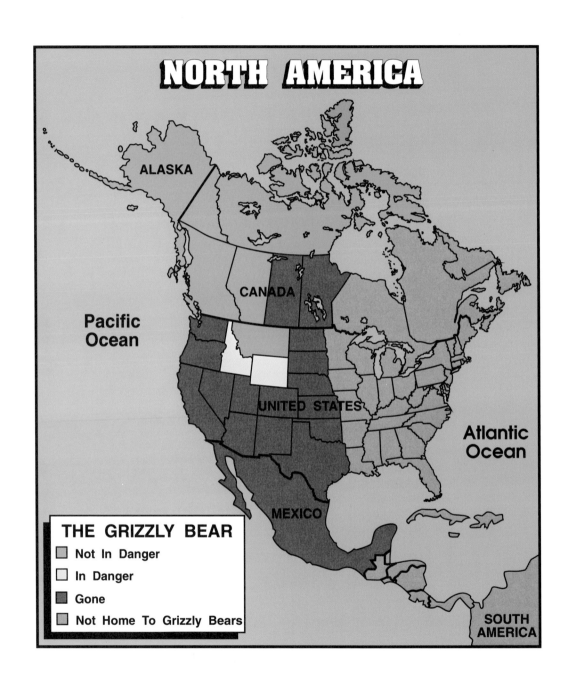

NORTH AMERICA

ALASKA

CANADA

Pacific
Ocean

UNITED STATES

Atlantic
Ocean

MEXICO

THE GRIZZLY BEAR

- ☐ Not In Danger
- ☐ In Danger
- ☐ Gone
- ☐ Not Home To Grizzly Bears

SOUTH
AMERICA

MORE FACTS ABOUT THE GRIZZLY BEAR

- Grizzlies are part of a group called brown bears.

- The male is called a boar. The female is called a sow.

- Sows usually have two cubs every two to three years. They are born in the den during the winter.

- Grizzlies have a big hump on their back near their shoulders.

- Grizzlies eat plants, insects, fish and dead animals. If they are very hungry, they will kill an animal.

- Most male grizzlies live alone. Females live with their cubs. Sometimes females become friends.

- Grizzlies can live 30 or more years, but most do not.

WORDS TO LEARN

boar—A male bear.

brown bears—A group of bears that includes the grizzly bear.

cub—A baby bear.

den—A resting place for animals. For grizzlies, it is a small room dug out of a hillside where grizzlies spend the winter.

grizzly bear—A large bear with a hump on it back. Its Latin name is *Ursus arctos horribilis*.

hibernate— To spend the winter in a deep sleep. The body works more slowly during hibernation. Grizzlies do not hibernate.

sow—A female bear.

INDEX